One-Dish Meals

Easy Everyday Recipe Library

BETTER HOMES AND GARDENS® BOOKS
Des Moines, Iowa

EASY EVERYDAY RECIPE LIBRARY

Better Homes and Gardens® Books, An imprint of Meredith® Books

Published for Creative World Enterprises LP, West Chester, Pennsylvania

www.creativeworldcooking.com

One-Dish Meals

Project Editors: Spectrum Communication Services, Inc.

Project Designers: Seif Visual Communications

Copy Chief: Catherine Hamrick

Copy and Production Editor: Terri Fredrickson

Contributing Proofreaders: Kathy Eastman, Susan J. Kling

Electronic Production Coordinator: Paula Forest

Editorial and Design Assistants: Judy Bailey, Mary Lee Gavin, Karen Schirm

Test Kitchen Director: Lynn Blanchard

Production Director: Douglas M. Johnston

Production Managers: Pam Kvitne, Marjorie J. Schenkelberg

Meredith® Books

Editor in Chief: James D. Blume

Design Director: Matt Strelecki

Managing Editor: Gregory H. Kayko

Director, Sales & Marketing, Retail: Michael A. Peterson

Director, Sales & Marketing, Special Markets: Rita McMullen

Director, Sales & Marketing, Home & Garden Center Channel: Ray Wolf

Director, Operations: George A. Susral

Vice President, General Manager: Jamie L. Martin

Better Homes and Gardens® Magazine

Editor in Chief: Jean LemMon

Executive Food Editor: Nancy Byal

Meredith Publishing Group

President, Publishing Group: Christopher M. Little

Vice President, Consumer Marketing & Development: Hal Oringer

Meredith Corporation

Chairman and Chief Executive Officer: William T. Kerr

Chairman of the Executive Committee: E. T. Meredith III

Creative World Enterprises LP

Publisher: Richard J. Petrone

Design Consultants to Creative World Enterprises: Coastline Studios, Orlando, Florida

All of us at Better Homes and Gardens® Books are dedicated to providing you with the information and ideas you need to create delicious foods. We welcome your comments and suggestions. Write to us at: Better Homes and Gardens Books, Cookbook Editorial Department, 1716 Locust St., Des Moines, Iowa 50309-3023.

Our seal assures you that every recipe in *One-Dish Meals* has been tested in the Better Homes and Gardens® Test Kitchen. This means that each recipe is practical and reliable, and meets our high standards of taste appeal. We guarantee your satisfaction with this book for as long as you own it.

Cover photo: Deep-Dish Chicken Pie
(see recipe, page 29)

Simplifying your life—that's what *One-Dish Meals* is all about. A meal you can serve in one dish makes for easy menu planning and no-fuss cleanup. Just add a salad or bread, and your meal is complete.

And what a meal it is. You'll find loads of tempting stir-fries, casseroles, skillet dishes, stews, pizzas, salads, and sandwiches in this tasty collection of one-dish recipes. And after dinner, your cleanup crew will appreciate recipes that you can often mix, cook, and serve in one dish.

CONTENTS

Zippy Beef, Mac and Cheese

Zippy Beef, Mac, and Cheese

For a fresh, pretty salad side dish, peel and section oranges and cut jicama into strips; arrange on a lettuce leaf and drizzle with an oil-and-vinegar dressing.

6   ounces packaged dried elbow
      macaroni or corkscrew macaroni
      (about 1½ cups)
12 ounces lean ground beef, pork,
      or raw turkey
1   15-ounce can tomato sauce
1   14½-ounce can stewed tomatoes or
      Mexican-style stewed tomatoes
4   ounces American or sharp American
      cheese, cut into small cubes
1   tablespoon chili powder
      Finely shredded or grated Parmesan
      cheese

In a 3-quart saucepan cook pasta according to package directions. Drain; keep warm. Meanwhile, in a large skillet cook ground meat till meat is brown. Drain fat.

Stir ground meat, tomato sauce, undrained tomatoes, cheese, and chili powder into cooked pasta. Cook and stir over medium heat for 6 to 8 minutes or till heated through. Sprinkle each serving with Parmesan cheese. Makes 4 servings.

Nutrition information per serving: 342 calories, 20 g protein, 32 g carbohydrate, 15 g fat (7 g saturated), 55 mg cholesterol, 957 mg sodium.

Easy Shepherd's Pie

Frozen mashed potatoes make quick work of this family-style skillet supper.

1   28-ounce package frozen mashed
        potatoes
1¾   cups milk
1   10-ounce package frozen mixed
        vegetables
1   pound ground beef, ground raw
        turkey, or ground raw chicken
¼   cup water
1   teaspoon dried minced onion
1   10¾-ounce can condensed tomato
        soup
1   teaspoon Worcestershire sauce
¼   teaspoon dried thyme, crushed
½   cup shredded cheddar cheese
        (2 ounces)

Prepare the potatoes according to package directions using 4 cups of the frozen potatoes and the milk. Meanwhile, run cold water over frozen vegetables to separate. In a large skillet cook ground meat till brown. Drain any fat. Stir in vegetables, water, and onion.

Bring to boiling; reduce heat. Cover and simmer for 5 to 10 minutes or till vegetables are tender. Stir in soup, Worcestershire, and thyme. Return to boiling. Drop potatoes in mounds on top of hot mixture. Sprinkle with cheese. Cover and simmer about 5 minutes or till heated through. Makes 6 servings.

Nutrition information per serving: 342 calories, 19 g protein, 30 g carbohydrate, 16 g fat (7 g saturated), 62 mg cholesterol, 541 mg sodium.

Ginger and Molasses Beef Stew

You can avoid an early-morning rush by doing some of the food prep the night before. Brown the meat, wrap in foil, and chill. Slice the vegetables and mix the ingredients for the tomato mixture, then chill separately. The next morning, combine the ingredients in the crockery cooker as directed in the recipe.

2 pounds lean beef stew meat, cut into 1-inch pieces
1 tablespoon cooking oil
4 carrots, sliced
2 medium parsnips, sliced
1 large onion, sliced
1 stalk celery, sliced
1 ¼-inch slice gingerroot or ½ teaspoon ground ginger
¼ cup quick-cooking tapioca
1 14½-ounce can diced tomatoes
¼ cup vinegar
¼ cup molasses
1 teaspoon salt
½ teaspoon pepper
½ cup raisins

In a large skillet brown the meat, a third at a time, in hot oil. Drain any fat.

In a 3½- to 6-quart crockery cooker place carrots, parsnips, onion, celery, and gingerroot (if using). Sprinkle tapioca over vegetables. Place meat in cooker. Combine undrained tomatoes, vinegar, molasses, salt, pepper, and ground ginger (if using); pour over meat.

Cover and cook on low-heat setting for 9 to 10 hours or on high-heat setting for 4 to 5 hours. Stir in raisins; cover and cook for 30 minutes more. Remove slice of gingerroot (if used). Makes 6 to 8 servings.

Nutrition information per serving: 564 calories, 40 g protein, 58 g carbohydrate, 19 g fat (5 g saturated), 110 mg cholesterol, 962 mg sodium.

Peppery Pot Roast

Your family might dub this "pot roast with pizazz" thanks to the black pepper, red pepper, and hot pepper sauce. Any meat leftovers will make tasty sandwiches on hearty rye bread.

1 2½- to 3-pound boneless beef chuck pot roast
1 teaspoon ground black pepper
½ teaspoon ground red pepper
2 tablespoons cooking oil
¾ cup vegetable juice
4 cloves garlic, halved
1 teaspoon instant beef bouillon granules
½ to 1 teaspoon bottled hot pepper sauce
½ teaspoon dry mustard
2 medium sweet potatoes, peeled and quartered
8 small parsnips, halved crosswise
4 stalks celery, bias-sliced into 1-inch pieces (2 cups)
1 medium onion, cut into wedges
½ cup cold water
¼ cup all-purpose flour
   Salt

Trim fat from meat. Rub black pepper and red pepper over meat. In a 4½-quart Dutch oven brown meat on all sides in hot oil. Drain fat. Combine vegetable juice, garlic, bouillon granules, pepper sauce, and mustard; pour over meat. Bring to boiling; reduce heat. Cover and simmer for 1 hour.

Add sweet potatoes, parsnips, celery, and onion. Cover and simmer for 45 to 60 minutes more or till meat is tender. Add water, if necessary, during cooking. Remove meat and vegetables from pan.

For gravy, skim fat from pan juices; measure juices and, if necessary, add enough water to equal 1½ cups. Combine the ½ cup cold water and flour. Stir into juices; return to pan. Cook and stir till thickened and bubbly. Cook and stir for 1 minute more. Season to taste with salt. Slice meat. Serve gravy with meat and vegetables. Makes 8 to 10 servings.

Nutrition information per serving: *485 calories, 50 g protein, 33 g carbohydrate, 16 g fat (6 g saturated), 143 mg cholesterol, 372 mg sodium.*

Southwestern Stuffed Pizza

For a doubly delicious taste, this robust pizza packs a zesty meat and corn filling between two crusts.

1½ pounds ground beef
1 12-ounce jar salsa
1 8¾-ounce can whole kernel corn, drained
1½ cups shredded cheddar cheese (6 ounces)
½ cup sliced pitted ripe olives
2 to 3 tablespoons snipped cilantro
¾ teaspoon ground cumin
¼ teaspoon pepper
1 16-ounce package hot roll mix
¼ cup cornmeal
½ teaspoon ground cumin
1 beaten egg

For filling, in a large skillet cook ground beef till brown. Drain fat. Stir in salsa, corn, cheese, olives, cilantro, the ¾ teaspoon cumin, and pepper. Set aside.

Prepare hot roll mix according to package directions, except stir the cornmeal and the ½ teaspoon cumin into the flour mixture and increase hot tap water to 1¼ cups. Turn dough out onto a lightly floured surface. Knead about 5 minutes or till smooth and elastic. Divide in half. Cover and let rest for 5 minutes.

Meanwhile, grease an 11- to 13-inch pizza pan. If desired, sprinkle with additional cornmeal. On a lightly floured surface, roll each half of dough into a circle 1 inch larger than pizza pan. Transfer one crust to pan. Spread meat mixture over dough.

Cut several slits in remaining crust. Place top crust on meat mixture. Trim and flute edge. Brush with beaten egg. If desired, sprinkle with additional cornmeal.

Bake in a 375° oven for 30 to 35 minutes or till crust is golden and pizza is heated through. If necessary, cover with foil after 20 minutes to prevent overbrowning. Makes 6 servings.

Nutrition information per serving: 724 calories, 42 g protein, 69 g carbohydrate, 31 g fat (12 g saturated), 171 mg cholesterol, 1,305 mg sodium.

Greek-Style Beef with Vegetables

Cinnamon, cloves, brown sugar, vinegar, and tomato paste give this fast-fix wok dish the distinctive flavor of Stefado (Greek beef stew).

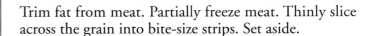

12	ounces beef top round steak or lean boneless lamb
3	medium potatoes, cut into ¾-inch cubes (3 cups)
2	medium carrots, bias-sliced (1 cup)
1	cup water
1	tablespoon cornstarch
1	tablespoon brown sugar
¾	teaspoon salt
½	teaspoon ground cinnamon
¼	teaspoon pepper
⅛	teaspoon ground cloves
½	of a 6-ounce can (⅓ cup) tomato paste
½	cup pitted ripe olives
1	tablespoon cooking oil
2	cloves garlic, minced
2	medium onions, cut into wedges
1	medium green, red, or yellow sweet pepper, cut into strips
2	tablespoons red wine vinegar

Trim fat from meat. Partially freeze meat. Thinly slice across the grain into bite-size strips. Set aside.

In a covered medium saucepan cook the potatoes and carrots in enough boiling water to cover about 10 minutes or just till tender. Drain. Set aside.

For sauce, in a small bowl stir together the water, cornstarch, brown sugar, salt, cinnamon, pepper, and cloves. Stir in tomato paste. Add olives. Set aside.

Add cooking oil to a wok or large skillet. Preheat over medium-high heat (add more oil if necessary during cooking). Stir-fry garlic in hot oil for 15 seconds. Add onions; stir-fry for 1 minute. Add sweet pepper; stir-fry about 2 minutes or till crisp-tender. Remove pepper mixture from wok.

Add meat to wok. Stir-fry for 2 to 3 minutes or to desired doneness. Push meat from center of wok.

Stir sauce; add to center of wok. Cook and stir till thickened and bubbly. Stir in vinegar. Return pepper mixture to wok. Add cooked potatoes and carrots. Stir to coat. Cover and cook for 1 to 2 minutes more or till heated through. Serve immediately. Makes 4 servings.

Nutrition information per serving: 376 calories, 26 g protein, 48 g carbohydrate, 11 g fat (2 g saturated fat), 54 mg cholesterol, 568 mg sodium.

Southwest Beef-Linguine Toss

A jar of picante sauce makes an easy, yet flavor-packed sauce in this one-dish meal.

4   ounces packaged dried linguine
12 ounces beef top round steak
1   tablespoon cooking oil
2   teaspoons chili powder
1   clove garlic, minced
1   small onion, sliced and separated
     into rings
1   red or green sweet pepper, cut into
     strips
1   10-ounce package frozen whole
     kernel corn
¼   cup picante sauce
     Cilantro sprigs (optional)

Cook pasta according to package directions. Drain pasta; rinse with warm water. Drain again. Meanwhile, trim fat from meat. Cut meat into thin, bite-size strips.

Add cooking oil to a wok or large skillet. Preheat over medium-high heat (add more oil if necessary during cooking). Stir-fry chili powder and garlic in hot oil for 15 seconds. Add onion; stir-fry for 1 minute. Add sweet pepper; stir-fry for 1 to 2 minutes more or till vegetables are crisp-tender. Remove from wok.

Add meat to wok. Stir-fry for 2 to 3 minutes or to desired doneness. Return vegetables to wok. Stir in corn and picante sauce. Add the cooked pasta. Toss all ingredients together to coat. Cook and stir till heated through. Serve immediately If desired, garnish with cilantro. Makes 4 servings.

Nutrition information per serving: 351 calories, 27 g protein, 43 g carbohydrate, 9 g fat (2 g saturated fat), 54 mg cholesterol, 166 mg sodium.

Deep-Dish Pizza

This substantial, two-crust pizza first became popular in Chicago back in the early 1940s.

1   16-ounce package hot roll mix
1   pound ground beef
1   cup chopped onion
2   cloves garlic, minced
1   8-ounce can pizza sauce
1   7-ounce jar roasted red sweet
      peppers, drained and chopped
1   4-ounce can sliced mushrooms,
      drained
1½ cups shredded provolone cheese
      (6 ounces)
1   10-ounce package frozen chopped
      spinach, thawed and well drained
1   slightly beaten egg

Prepare hot roll mix according to package directions through the kneading step. Cover and let rest.

Meanwhile, in a large skillet cook ground beef, onion, and garlic till meat is brown and onion is tender. Drain fat. Stir in pizza sauce, red peppers, and mushrooms; heat through. Cover and keep warm.

Grease the bottom of a 9-inch springform pan. On a lightly floured surface, roll three-fourths of the dough into a 13-inch circle. Fit into the bottom and press up the side of the springform pan. Sprinkle bottom of dough with ½ cup of the provolone cheese. Spoon meat mixture over cheese.

Pat spinach dry with paper towels. Combine spinach, egg, and remaining provolone cheese. Spread spinach mixture over meat mixture. Roll remaining dough into a 9-inch circle; place on spinach mixture. Fold excess bottom dough under; pinch to seal.

Bake in a 350° oven for 40 to 45 minutes or till golden brown. Cool on a wire rack for 10 minutes. To serve, remove side of springform pan; cut into wedges. Makes 8 servings.

Nutrition information per serving: 480 calories, 27 g protein, 53 g carbohydrate, 18 g fat (7 g saturated), 102 mg cholesterol, 804 mg sodium.

Warm Thai Beef Salad

Be sure to use hot bean paste, not a milder bean sauce, to get the maximum heat from this main dish salad. Look for bean paste at large supermarkets, specialty food stores, or Asian markets.

12 ounces beef flank steak
¼ cup plum sauce
2 tablespoons red wine vinegar
1 tablespoon water
1 to 2 teaspoons hot bean paste
¼ to ½ teaspoon crushed red pepper
4 cups torn mixed greens (such as curly endive, spinach, arugula, radicchio, watercress, and/or leaf lettuce)
1 11-ounce can mandarin oranges, drained
2 tablespoons cooking oil
1 red sweet pepper, cut into strips
1 yellow sweet pepper, cut into strips
3 serrano chili peppers, seeded and finely chopped
1 clove garlic, minced

Trim fat from meat. Partially freeze meat. Thinly slice across the grain into bite-size strips. For sauce, in a small mixing bowl stir together plum sauce, vinegar, water, hot bean paste, and red pepper; set aside.

Arrange mixed greens and mandarin oranges on individual serving plates; set aside.

Add 1 tablespoon cooking oil to a wok or large skillet. Preheat over medium-high heat. Stir-fry the sweet peppers, chili peppers, and garlic in hot oil for 3 to 4 minutes or till sweet peppers are crisp-tender. Remove peppers from wok.

Add remaining oil to wok. Add meat; stir-fry for 2 to 3 minutes or to desired doneness. Stir in sauce. Return cooked peppers to wok. Cook and stir about 2 minutes more or till heated through.

Spoon meat mixture over greens mixture on plates. Serve warm. Makes 4 servings.

Nutrition information per serving: 283 calories, 21 g protein, 18 g carbohydrate, 17 g fat (4 g saturated), 40 mg cholesterol, 177 mg sodium.

Curried Pork Stew

Look for chili oil (also called hot oil or hot pepper oil) in the Oriental section of your supermarket, at an Oriental market, or a specialty food store. If you use cooking oil instead of chili oil, then increase the ground red pepper to ¼ teaspoon.

12 ounces lean boneless pork
1 medium onion, chopped (½ cup)
2 cloves garlic, minced
1 tablespoon chili oil or cooking oil
1 tablespoon curry powder
1 teaspoon grated gingerroot
⅛ teaspoon ground red pepper
¼ cup water
1 tablespoon all-purpose flour
1 14½-ounce can diced tomatoes
2 medium carrots, sliced
1 medium sweet potato, peeled and
   cut into bite-size pieces
¼ cup mixed dried fruit bits
   Salt
¼ cup snipped parsley
¼ cup chopped peanuts

Trim fat from meat. Cut meat into ¾-inch cubes. In a large skillet cook meat, onion, and garlic in hot oil over medium-high heat till meat is brown and onion is tender. Stir in the curry powder, gingerroot, and red pepper. Cook and stir for 1 minute more.

In a 2-quart round casserole stir together water and flour. Add undrained tomatoes, carrots, sweet potato, and dried fruit bits. Add meat mixture; mix well.

Cover and bake in a 350° oven about 1 hour or till meat is tender. If desired, season to taste with salt. To serve, sprinkle each serving with parsley and peanuts. Makes 4 servings.

Nutrition information per serving: 324 calories, 18 g protein, 30 g carbohydrate, 16 g fat (4 g saturated), 44 mg cholesterol, 450 mg sodium.

Pork and Noodle Skillet Dinner

Strips of boneless chicken breasts or thighs taste equally delicious in this creamy one-dish meal.

12 ounces lean boneless pork
 1 medium onion, chopped (½ cup)
 1 tablespoon cooking oil
 3 cups frozen loose-pack broccoli,
       cauliflower, and carrots
 4 ounces packaged dried medium
       noodles or curly medium noodles
       (3 cups)
 1 10¾-ounce can reduced-sodium
       condensed cream of celery soup
 1 cup reduced-sodium chicken broth
 ¾ cup water
 ½ teaspoon dried marjoram or thyme,
       crushed
 ¼ teaspoon pepper

Trim fat from meat. Cut meat into thin bite-size strips. In a 12-inch skillet cook and stir meat and onion in hot oil over medium-high heat for 3 to 4 minutes or till meat is brown.

Stir in frozen vegetables, noodles, soup, broth, water, marjoram or thyme, and pepper. Bring to boiling; reduce heat. Cover and simmer for 12 to 15 minutes or till noodles are tender, stirring occasionally. Makes 4 servings.

Nutrition information per serving: 317 calories, 19 g protein, 33 g carbohydrate, 12 g fat (3 g saturated), 64 mg cholesterol, 531 mg sodium.

Pork & Mushroom Pasta Pizza

A pasta crust makes this pizza different from all the rest.

2 cups packaged dried rope macaroni (gemelli) or corkscrew macaroni
1 slightly beaten egg
¼ cup milk
2 tablespoons grated Parmesan or Romano cheese
1 pound ground pork or ground beef
1 cup chopped onion
2 cloves garlic, minced
1 15-ounce can or one 15½-ounce jar pizza sauce
¼ teaspoon crushed red pepper
1 4-ounce can sliced mushrooms, drained
½ cup chopped green sweet pepper
1 cup shredded mozzarella cheese (4 ounces)

Cook pasta according to package directions. Drain pasta; rinse with cold water. Drain again. Combine egg, milk, and Parmesan or Romano cheese. Stir in pasta. Spread mixture evenly into a greased 13-inch pizza pan. Bake in a 350° oven for 20 minutes.

Meanwhile, in a large skillet cook ground meat, onion, and garlic till meat is brown and onion is tender. Drain fat. Stir in pizza sauce and crushed red pepper. Bring to boiling; reduce heat. Cover and simmer for 10 minutes. Spoon meat mixture over baked pasta crust. Top with the mushrooms and green pepper. Sprinkle with mozzarella cheese.

Bake for 10 to 12 minutes more or till cheese is melted and pizza is heated through. Makes 6 servings.

Nutrition information per serving: 331 calories, 21 g protein, 33 g carbohydrate, 13 g fat (3 g saturated), 83 mg cholesterol, 590 mg sodium.

White Bean and Sausage Rigatoni

Reminiscent of a wonderful baked Italian casserole that comes bubbling from the oven, this dish is done on the stovetop instead, so it's ready to put on the table in less than half the time. Snipped fresh basil adds a licorice like freshness.

8 ounces packaged dried rigatoni

1 15-ounce can white kidney (cannellini), great northern, or navy beans, rinsed and drained

1 14½-ounce can Italian-style stewed tomatoes

6 ounces light fully cooked smoked sausage or fully cooked smoked turkey sausage, sliced ½ inch thick

⅓ cup snipped fresh basil

¼ cup shaved or finely shredded Asiago cheese (1 ounce)

Cook pasta according to package directions, except do not add salt to cooking water. Drain; keep warm.

Meanwhile, in a large saucepan combine beans, undrained tomatoes, and sausage; heat through.

Add the bean mixture and basil to cooked pasta; toss gently to combine. Sprinkle each serving with Asiago cheese. Makes 4 servings.

Nutrition information per serving: 401 calories, 25 g protein, 67 g carbohydrate, 6 g fat (1 g saturated), 32 mg cholesterol, 964 mg sodium.

Beyond Red Kidney Beans

When you think of kidney beans, the red ones probably come to mind. But their Italian cousins, the cannellini beans, also are a versatile and delicious choice. These white, mild-tasting beans are ideal for making casseroles, soups, stews, and other one-dish meals, such as White Bean and Sausage Rigatoni (above). Cannellini come in both canned and dried forms. Look for them with the other canned or dried beans in your supermarket or at Italian food specialty stores.

Sausage and Cabbage Skillet

Fully cooked sausage links are an easy answer to dinner because they need only to be heated through. However, longer simmering, as is done in this recipe, sometimes is preferred to develop the flavor of a dish.

1 small head cabbage, shredded
    (5 cups), or 5 cups packaged
    shredded cabbage with carrot
    (coleslaw mix)
4 medium potatoes, sliced
1 medium onion, sliced and separated
    into rings
1 teaspoon caraway seed (optional)
1 pound fully cooked kielbasa or other
    smoked sausage links, halved
    lengthwise and bias-sliced into
    1-inch pieces
1 cup apple juice
2 tablespoons brown or prepared
    mustard
½ teaspoon instant beef bouillon
    granules

In a 12-inch skillet combine cabbage, sliced potatoes, onion, and, if desired, caraway seed. Top with the sausage pieces.

In a small mixing bowl combine apple juice, mustard, and bouillon granules. Pour over sausage mixture in skillet. Bring to boiling; reduce heat. Cover and simmer about 30 minutes or till vegetables are tender. Makes 5 servings.

Nutrition information per serving: *483 calories, 15 g protein, 43 g carbohydrate, 28 g fat (10 g saturated), 75 mg cholesterol, 1,041 mg sodium.*

Lamb and Bean Ragout

This saucy lamb dish gets a protein boost from a vegetable source—white kidney beans.

8 ounces lean boneless lamb or beef
    top round steak
8 ounces whole fresh mushrooms
1 tablespoon cooking oil
2 cloves garlic, minced
2 medium onions, cut into thin
    wedges
1 medium yellow summer squash,
    halved lengthwise and sliced
    (1¼ cups)
1 tablespoon snipped fresh basil or
    1 teaspoon dried basil, crushed
1 15- to 19-ounce can white kidney
    (cannellini) beans, rinsed and
    drained
1 14½-ounce can tomatoes, cut up
½ teaspoon salt
⅛ teaspoon pepper
8 ounces packaged dried rigatoni or
    cut ziti, cooked and drained
    Fresh basil sprigs (optional)

Trim fat from meat. Partially freeze meat. Thinly slice across the grain into bite-size strips. Cut any large mushrooms in half. Set aside.

Add cooking oil to a wok or large skillet. Preheat over medium-high heat (add more oil if necessary during cooking). Stir-fry garlic in hot oil for 15 seconds. Add onions; stir-fry for 3 minutes. Add mushrooms, squash, and snipped fresh or dried basil; stir-fry for 3 to 4 minutes or till vegetables are crisp-tender. Remove vegetables from wok.

Add meat to wok. Stir-fry for 2 to 3 minutes or to desired doneness. Return cooked vegetables to wok. Stir in beans, undrained tomatoes, salt, and pepper. Cook and stir for 3 to 4 minutes or till slightly thickened. Serve immediately over hot pasta. If desired, garnish with basil sprigs. Makes 4 to 5 servings.

Nutrition information per serving: 439 calories, 26 g protein, 73 g carbohydrate, 8 g fat (2 g saturated fat), 29 mg cholesterol, 644 mg sodium.

Greek-Style Pasta Skillet

Lamb, cinnamon, and feta cheese add a Greek twist to this macaroni casserole.

12 ounces ground lamb or ground beef
1 medium onion, chopped (½ cup)
1 14½-ounce can diced tomatoes
1 5½-ounce can tomato juice
½ cup water
½ teaspoon instant beef bouillon
   granules
½ teaspoon ground cinnamon
⅛ teaspoon garlic powder
1 cup packaged dried medium shell
   macaroni or elbow macaroni
1 cup loose-pack frozen cut green
   beans
½ cup crumbled feta cheese

In a large skillet cook ground meat and onion till meat is brown. Drain fat.

Stir in the undrained tomatoes, tomato juice, water, bouillon granules, cinnamon, and garlic powder. Bring to boiling.

Stir the uncooked pasta and green beans into meat mixture. Return to boiling; reduce heat. Cover and simmer about 15 minutes or till pasta and green beans are tender. Sprinkle with feta cheese. Makes 4 servings.

Nutrition information per serving: 362 calories, 22 g protein, 33 g carbohydrate, 16 g fat (7 g saturated fat), 70 mg cholesterol, 647 mg sodium.

Chicken, Pear, and Blue Cheese Salad

The pairing of pears and blue cheese is naturally fresh and simple. Combine this twosome with a package of assorted greens and rotisserie chicken from the deli, and you've got a dinner that's naturally elegant as well.

6 cups torn mixed greens or mesclun
   (about 8 ounces)
10 to 12 ounces roasted or grilled
   chicken breast, sliced
¾ cup bottled reduced-calorie or
   regular blue cheese salad dressing
2 ripe pears, cored and sliced
   Freshly ground pepper (optional)

In a large mixing bowl combine the mixed greens, chicken, and salad dressing; toss gently to coat.

Arrange greens mixture in individual salad bowls or on dinner plates. Top with pear slices. If desired, sprinkle with pepper. Makes 4 servings.

Nutrition information per serving: 208 calories, 23 g protein, 18 g carbohydrate, 6 g fat (2 g saturated fat), 72 mg cholesterol, 591 mg sodium.

Greek-Style Pasta Skillet

Deep-Dish Chicken Pie

To save time with the same delicious results, you can easily substitute one folded refrigerated unbaked piecrust for the Pastry for Single-Crust Pie. Just put the chicken mixture in a 2-quart round casserole and top with the piecrust. Flute, brush, and bake as directed in the recipe. (Also pictured on the cover.)

Pastry for Single-Crust Pie
- 3 medium leeks or 1 large onion, chopped
- 1 cup sliced fresh mushrooms
- ¾ cup sliced celery
- ½ cup chopped red sweet pepper
- 2 tablespoons margarine or butter
- ⅓ cup all-purpose flour
- 1 teaspoon poultry seasoning
- ¼ teaspoon salt
- ¼ teaspoon black pepper
- 1½ cups chicken broth
- 1 cup half-and-half, light cream, or milk
- 2½ cups chopped cooked chicken
- 1 cup frozen peas
- 1 slightly beaten egg

Prepare Pastry for Single-Crust Pie. On a lightly floured surface, roll pastry into a rectangle ⅛ inch thick. Trim to a rectangle 1 inch larger than a 2-quart rectangular baking dish. Using a sharp knife or small cookie cutter, cut some shapes out of center of pastry.

In a large saucepan cook leeks or onion, mushrooms, celery, and sweet pepper in margarine or butter over medium heat till tender. Stir in the flour, poultry seasoning, salt, and black pepper. Add the broth and half-and-half, light cream, or milk all at once. Cook and stir till thickened and bubbly. Stir in the cooked chicken and peas. Pour into the baking dish.

Place pastry over the hot chicken mixture in dish; turn edges of pastry under and flute to top edges of dish. Brush with the egg. Place reserved pastry shapes on top of pastry. Brush again with egg.

Bake in a 400° oven for 30 to 35 minutes or till the crust is golden brown. Cool about 20 minutes before serving. Makes 6 servings.

Pastry for Single-Crust Pie: In a medium bowl stir together 1¼ cups *all-purpose flour* and ¼ teaspoon *salt*. Using a pastry blender, cut in ⅓ cup *shortening* till pieces are pea-size. Using 4 to 5 tablespoons *cold water*, sprinkle 1 tablespoon water at a time over mixture, gently tossing with a fork till all is moistened. Form dough into a ball.

Nutrition information per serving: 484 calories, 27 g protein, 35 g carbohydrate, 26 g fat (8 g saturated fat), 107 mg cholesterol, 538 mg sodium.

Popover Pizza Casserole

For this homestyle dish, a saucy turkey and pepperoni mixture is topped with a layer of mozzarella cheese and a popover batter that puffs while it bakes.

1 pound ground raw turkey or ground beef
1 cup chopped onion
1 cup chopped green sweet pepper
1 15-ounce can or one 15½-ounce jar pizza sauce
1 2-ounce can mushroom stems and pieces, drained
½ of a 3½-ounce package sliced pepperoni, halved
½ teaspoon fennel seed, crushed
½ teaspoon dried oregano, crushed
½ teaspoon dried basil, crushed
2 eggs
1 cup milk
1 tablespoon cooking oil
1 cup all-purpose flour
1 6-ounce package thinly sliced mozzarella cheese
¼ cup grated Parmesan cheese

In a large skillet cook meat, onion, and green pepper till meat is brown and vegetables are tender. Drain fat. Stir in pizza sauce, mushrooms, pepperoni, fennel seed, oregano, and basil. Bring to boiling; reduce heat. Simmer, uncovered, for 10 minutes; stir occasionally.

Meanwhile, combine eggs, milk, and oil. Beat with an electric mixer on medium speed for 1 minute. Add flour; beat for 1 minute more or till smooth.

Grease sides of a 13x9x2-inch baking dish; spoon meat mixture into dish. Arrange cheese slices over hot meat mixture. Pour egg mixture over cheese, covering completely. Sprinkle with Parmesan cheese. Bake in a 400° oven for 25 to 30 minutes or till top is puffed and golden. Serve immediately. Makes 8 servings.

Nutrition information per serving: 316 calories, 21 g protein, 22 g carbohydrate, 16 g fat (6 g saturated), 91 mg cholesterol, 688 mg sodium.

Southwest Chicken Skillet

Serve this family-pleasing, one-dish meal with corn muffins and a tossed salad.

12 ounces skinless, boneless chicken
       breast halves
1   tablespoon cooking oil
1   15-ounce jar salsa
¾   cup chicken broth
½   cup chopped green sweet pepper
¼   cup sliced pitted ripe olives
       (optional)
1   cup quick-cooking rice
½   cup shredded cheddar or Monterey
       Jack cheese (2 ounces)
     Green sweet pepper strips (optional)

Rinse chicken; pat dry with paper towels. Cut chicken into 1-inch pieces. In a large skillet cook and stir chicken in hot oil over medium heat for 2 to 3 minutes or till tender and no longer pink.

Stir in salsa, chicken broth, chopped green pepper, and, if desired, olives. Bring to boiling. Stir in rice. Remove from heat. Sprinkle with cheese. Cover and let stand about 5 minutes or till rice is tender. If desired, garnish with green pepper strips. Makes 4 servings.

Nutrition information per serving: 344 calories, 25 g protein, 34 g carbohydrate, 15 g fat (4 g saturated), 60 mg cholesterol, 1,012 mg sodium.

Herbed Turkey and Broccoli

Soft-style cream cheese makes an ultra-rich sauce for this one-pan pasta dish.

8   ounces packaged dried linguine or
       spaghetti, broken in half
3   cups small broccoli flowerets
1   8-ounce container soft-style cream
       cheese with garlic and herbs
⅔   cup milk
¼   teaspoon coarsely ground pepper
6   ounces sliced fully cooked smoked
       turkey breast, cut into bite-size
       strips

In a 4½-quart Dutch oven cook pasta in boiling water for 6 minutes. Add broccoli. Return to boiling. Cook for 2 to 3 minutes more or till pasta is tender and broccoli is crisp-tender. Drain in a colander.

In the same Dutch oven combine cream cheese, milk, and pepper. Cook and stir over low heat till cream cheese is melted. Add pasta mixture and turkey. Toss to coat. If necessary, stir in additional milk to make desired consistency. Makes 4 servings.

Nutrition information per serving: 516 calories, 25 g protein, 57 g carbohydrate, 21 g fat (11 g saturated), 81 mg cholesterol, 675 mg sodium.

Turkey Tetrazzini

Tetrazzini is a quick supper when cooked in a wok—there's plenty of room for tossing the spaghetti with the meat, mushrooms, and creamy sauce.

12	ounces turkey breast tenderloin steaks
1⅔	cups milk
2	tablespoons all-purpose flour
2	teaspoons instant chicken bouillon granules
⅛	teaspoon pepper
¼	cup slivered almonds
1	tablespoon cooking oil
1	cup sliced fresh mushrooms
2	green onions, sliced (¼ cup)
2	tablespoons dry white wine, dry sherry, or milk
4	ounces packaged dried thin spaghetti, cooked and drained
¼	cup finely shredded Parmesan cheese
2	tablespoons snipped parsley
	Tomato slices (optional)
	Parsley sprigs (optional)

Rinse turkey; pat dry with paper towels. Cut into thin bite-size strips. For sauce, in a small bowl stir together 1⅔ cups milk, flour, bouillon granules, and pepper till smooth. Set aside.

Preheat a wok or large skillet over medium-high heat. Add almonds; stir-fry for 2 to 3 minutes or till golden. Remove almonds from wok. Let wok cool slightly.

Add cooking oil to cooled wok. Preheat over medium-high heat (add more oil if necessary during cooking). Stir-fry mushrooms and green onions in hot oil for 1 to 2 minutes or just till tender. Remove mushroom mixture from wok.

Add turkey to wok. Stir-fry for 2 to 3 minutes or till tender and no longer pink. Push turkey from center of wok. Stir sauce; add to center of wok. Cook and stir till thickened and bubbly. Cook and stir for 2 minutes more.

Stir in wine, sherry, or milk. Return the mushroom mixture to wok. Add cooked spaghetti, Parmesan cheese, and parsley. Toss to coat. Cook and stir for 1 to 2 minutes more or till heated through. Sprinkle with toasted almonds. Serve immediately. If desired, garnish with tomato and parsley. Makes 4 servings.

Nutrition information per serving: 376 calories, 28 g protein, 34 g carbohydrate, 13 g fat (4 g saturated fat), 50 mg cholesterol, 637 mg sodium.

Easy Salmon Pasta

To save time, we cook the pasta and vegetables together in the same pan.

2 cups frozen loose-pack mixed
    vegetables or one 10-ounce
    package frozen mixed vegetables
1½ cups packaged dried corkscrew
    macaroni
2 green onions, sliced (¼ cup)
1 10¾-ounce can condensed cheddar
    cheese soup
½ cup milk
½ teaspoon dried dillweed
¼ teaspoon dry mustard
⅛ teaspoon pepper
2 6-ounce cans skinless, boneless
    salmon or tuna, drained
    Fresh dill (optional)

In a large saucepan cook frozen vegetables, pasta, and green onions in boiling water for 10 to 12 minutes or just till pasta is tender. Drain well.

Stir soup, milk, dried dillweed, mustard, and pepper into pasta mixture. Gently fold in salmon or tuna. Cook over low heat till heated through. If desired, garnish with fresh dill. Makes 5 servings.

Nutrition information per serving: 347 calories, 22 g protein, 41 g carbohydrate, 9 g fat (4 g saturated fat), 56 mg cholesterol, 827 mg sodium.

No-Chop Scallop Stir-Fry

Scallops are available in two sizes. Bay scallops measure about ½ inch in diameter and sea scallops about 1½ inches. Both are delicious in this easy stir-fry dish, but cut the large scallops in half before cooking.

8   ounces Chinese egg noodles or
        packaged dried vermicelli, broken
        into 3- to 4-inch pieces
¼   cup soy sauce
3   tablespoons dry sherry or apple juice
½   teaspoon ground ginger
12 ounces fresh bay or sea scallops
1   tablespoon cooking oil
3   cloves garlic, minced
2   cups loose-pack frozen stir-fry
        vegetables

In a large saucepan cook egg noodles in boiling water for 3 to 4 minutes or just till tender. (Or, cook the vermicelli according to package directions.) Drain pasta; rinse with hot water. Drain again.

Meanwhile, for sauce, in a small bowl stir together soy sauce, sherry or apple juice, and ginger. Cut any large scallops in half. Set aside.

Add cooking oil to a wok or large skillet. Preheat over medium-high heat (add more oil if necessary during cooking). Stir-fry the garlic in hot oil for 15 seconds. Add frozen vegetables. Stir-fry for 2 to 3 minutes or till crisp-tender. Remove the vegetables from wok.

Add scallops to wok. Stir-fry for 2 to 3 minutes or till scallops are opaque. Add cooked noodles, vegetables, and sauce to wok. Toss all ingredients together to coat. Cook and stir till heated through. Serve immediately. Makes 4 servings.

Nutrition information per serving: 285 calories, 18 g protein, 37 g carbohydrate, 6 g fat (1 g saturated), 62 mg cholesterol, 1,178 mg sodium.

Seafood Lasagna

Treat yourself to a version of lasagna that's even more indulgent than the traditional one.

½ cup frozen, peeled, cooked shrimp or one 4-ounce can shrimp, drained
1 8-ounce package chunk-style imitation crabmeat
2 14½-ounce cans stewed tomatoes, cut up
½ cup sliced fresh mushrooms
½ teaspoon onion powder
½ teaspoon dried oregano, crushed
Dash salt
Dash pepper
3 tablespoons margarine or butter
3 tablespoons all-purpose flour
1¾ cups milk
1 cup shredded Swiss cheese (4 ounces)
¼ cup dry white wine
8 packaged dried lasagna noodles, cooked and drained
¼ cup grated Romano or Parmesan cheese
Fresh oregano (optional)

Thaw shrimp, if frozen. If necessary, cut crabmeat into bite-size pieces. Rinse shrimp and crabmeat; pat dry with paper towels. Set aside.

For shrimp sauce, in a medium saucepan combine undrained tomatoes, mushrooms, onion powder, dried oregano, salt, and pepper. Bring to boiling; reduce heat. Simmer, uncovered, about 20 minutes or till mixture is thickened. Remove from heat. Stir in shrimp. Set aside.

For cheese sauce, in a medium saucepan melt the margarine or butter over medium heat. Stir in flour. Add milk all at once. Cook and stir till thickened and bubbly. Cook and stir for 1 minute more. Add Swiss cheese, stirring till melted. Stir in crabmeat and wine.

In an 11x7x1½-inch baking dish layer half of the shrimp sauce, half of the lasagna noodles, and half of the cheese sauce. Repeat layers. Sprinkle with Romano or Parmesan cheese. Bake, uncovered, in a 350° oven about 25 minutes or till heated through. Let stand for 15 minutes before serving. If desired, garnish with fresh oregano. Makes 6 to 8 servings.

Nutrition information per serving: 347 calories, 20 g protein, 33 g carbohydrate, 15 g fat (6 g saturated), 58 mg cholesterol, 925 mg sodium.

Shrimp with Peppers and Corn

Because jalapeño peppers contain volatile oils that can burn your skin and eyes, avoid direct contact with the peppers. When seeding and chopping them wear plastic or rubber gloves or work under cold running water. If your bare hands touch the peppers, wash them well with soap and water.

1½ pounds fresh or frozen peeled, deveined medium or jumbo shrimp

1 cup water

1 teaspoon instant chicken bouillon granules

2 cups fresh corn or frozen corn, thawed

1 large red or green sweet pepper, chopped (1 cup)

2 to 4 cloves garlic, minced

1 tablespoon cooking oil

¼ cup dry white wine

2 tablespoons lemon juice

1 jalapeño pepper, seeded and finely chopped

1 teaspoon cornstarch

½ teaspoon dried oregano, crushed

¼ teaspoon salt

⅛ to ¼ teaspoon ground red pepper

⅛ teaspoon ground cumin
Jalapeño peppers (optional)

Thaw shrimp, if frozen. Rinse shrimp; pat dry with paper towels. Set aside.

In a large skillet combine water and chicken bouillon granules. Bring to boiling. Add shrimp. Return to boiling; reduce heat. Cover and simmer for 1 to 3 minutes or till shrimp turn pink. Drain shrimp in a colander; set aside.

In the same skillet cook corn, sweet pepper, and garlic in hot oil about 3 minutes or till corn is tender, stirring often. Set aside.

In a small bowl stir together white wine, lemon juice, finely chopped jalapeño pepper, cornstarch, oregano, salt, ground red pepper, and cumin. Stir wine mixture into the vegetable mixture in skillet. Cook and stir till thickened and bubbly.

Return shrimp to skillet. Cook about 2 minutes more or till mixture is heated through, stirring gently. If desired, garnish with whole jalapeño peppers. Makes 4 to 6 servings.

Nutrition information per serving: 272 calories, 31 g protein, 23 g carbohydrate, 6 g fat (1 g saturated), 261 mg cholesterol, 501 mg sodium.

Simple Seafood Gumbo

Ready-to-go products like Cajun-style stewed tomatoes and cooked seafood make everything simple and foolproof in this hearty gumbo.

1	medium green sweet pepper, chopped (1 cup)
1	medium onion, chopped (½ cup)
1	tablespoon cooking oil
1	tablespoon cornstarch
1	14½-ounce can Cajun-style stewed tomatoes
2	6-ounce cans (1½ cups) hot-style tomato juice
½	of a 10-ounce package frozen cut okra (1 cup)
1	8-ounce package frozen, peeled, cooked shrimp
½	of an 8-ounce package flake-style imitation crabmeat (about 1 cup)
¾	cup quick-cooking rice
½	cup beef broth

In a large saucepan cook green pepper and onion in hot oil till tender. Stir in cornstarch. Add undrained stewed tomatoes and tomato juice. Cook and stir till thickened and bubbly.

Stir in okra. Bring to boiling; reduce heat. Cover and simmer for 10 minutes.

Stir in shrimp, crabmeat, rice, and beef broth. Return to boiling; remove from heat. Cover and let stand about 5 minutes or till the rice is tender, stirring occasionally. Makes 4 servings.

Nutrition information per serving: 259 calories, 20 g protein, 35 g carbohydrate, 5 g fat (1 g saturated), 116 mg cholesterol, 1,132 mg sodium.

Clam and Bacon Bundles

Brushing the bundles with milk before baking makes them even more crispy and irresistibly golden brown.

2 slices bacon, cut up
¾ cup finely chopped broccoli
    (4 to 5 ounces)
1 medium carrot, shredded (½ cup)
1 small yellow summer squash,
    chopped (1 cup)
2 6½-ounce cans chopped clams,
    drained
⅓ cup soft-style cream cheese with
    chives and onion
2 tablespoons creamy cucumber
    salad dressing
1 10-ounce package refrigerated
    pizza dough
1 tablespoon milk
1 tablespoon sesame seed

In a large skillet cook bacon till crisp. Remove bacon, reserving 1 tablespoon drippings in skillet. Drain bacon on paper towels. For filling, cook broccoli and carrot in reserved drippings for 2 minutes. Add squash; cook for 1 minute more. Remove from heat. Stir in clams, cream cheese, salad dressing, and bacon.

On a lightly floured surface, roll pizza dough into a 12-inch square. Cut dough into four 6-inch squares. Place ½ cup of the filling on one corner of each square. Moisten edges and fold opposite corner over filling. Press edges with tines of fork to seal. Brush bundles with milk. Sprinkle with sesame seed.

Place on a greased baking sheet. Bake in a 400° oven about 20 minutes or till golden. Cool on a wire rack for 5 minutes. Serve warm. Makes 4 servings.

Nutrition information per serving: 390 calories, 23 g protein, 35 g carbohydrate, 18 g fat (5 g saturated), 57 mg cholesterol, 494 mg sodium.

Mexican Black Bean Pizza

The beans and cheese provide more than enough protein in this meatless pizza.

1   10-ounce package refrigerated
    pizza dough
1   15-ounce can black beans, rinsed
    and drained
2   tablespoons snipped cilantro or
    parsley
2   tablespoons salsa
2   cloves garlic, quartered
1   teaspoon ground cumin
¼   teaspoon bottled hot pepper sauce
1½ cups shredded Cojack or cheddar
    cheese (6 ounces)
½   cup chopped red sweet pepper
¼   cup sliced green onions
½   cup dairy sour cream
2   tablespoons salsa

Lightly grease an 11- to 13-inch pizza pan. Unroll pizza dough and transfer to greased pan, pressing dough out with your hands. Build up edge slightly. Prick generously with a fork. Bake in a 425° oven for 7 to 10 minutes or till lightly browned.

Meanwhile, in a blender container or food processor bowl combine the black beans, cilantro or parsley, 2 tablespoons salsa, garlic, cumin, and hot pepper sauce. Cover and blend or process till smooth, stopping to scrape down sides if necessary.

Spread bean mixture over hot crust. Sprinkle with Cojack or cheddar cheese, red sweet pepper, and green onions. Bake about 10 minutes more or till cheese is melted and pizza is heated through.

In a small bowl combine sour cream and 2 tablespoons salsa. Serve pizza with sour cream mixture. Makes 4 servings.

Nutrition information per serving: 468 calories, 24 g protein, 51 g carbohydrate, 20 g fat (11 g saturated), 50 mg cholesterol, 917 mg sodium.

Pizza Dough Pointer

If you don't have refrigerated pizza dough on hand or it's not available at your supermarket, you can prepare your own pizza dough for Mexican Black Bean Pizza (above) from a favorite recipe or from a mix. You'll need enough dough to fit an 11- to 13-inch pizza pan.

Italian Three-Bean and Rice Skillet

Red beans, lima beans, and green beans comprise the basil-scented trio.

1   15- to 15½-ounce can small red
     beans or red kidney beans, rinsed
     and drained
1   14½-ounce can Italian-style stewed
     tomatoes, cut up
1   cup vegetable broth or chicken
     broth
¾   cup quick-cooking brown rice
½   of a 10-ounce package frozen baby
     lima beans
½   of a 9-ounce package frozen cut
     green beans
½   teaspoon dried basil or Italian
     seasoning, crushed
1   cup meatless spaghetti sauce
2   ounces thinly sliced mozzarella
     cheese or ¼ cup grated Parmesan
     cheese (optional)

In a large skillet combine red beans or kidney beans, undrained tomatoes, broth, rice, lima beans, green beans, and basil or Italian seasoning. Bring to boiling; reduce heat. Cover and simmer about 15 minutes or till rice is tender.

Stir in spaghetti sauce. Heat through. If desired, top with mozzarella or Parmesan cheese. Makes 4 servings.

Nutrition information per serving: 259 calories, 14 g protein, 50 g carbohydrate, 4 g fat (0 g saturated), 0 mg cholesterol, 1,103 mg sodium.

Pasta with Garden Vegetables

Two kinds of Italian cheese, Romano and provolone, combine with corkscrew macaroni and an array
of fresh vegetables to create supper for four or side-dish servings for half a dozen.

1   tablespoon cooking oil
1   clove garlic, minced
2   small zucchini, sliced ¼ inch
    thick (2 cups)
1   small yellow summer squash,
    sliced ¼ inch thick (1 cup)
2   cups sliced fresh mushrooms
3   green onions, sliced (⅓ cup)
1   large tomato, chopped (1½ cups)
½   teaspoon dried oregano, crushed
⅛   teaspoon pepper
8   ounces packaged dried corkscrew
    macaroni, cooked and drained
¼   cup finely shredded Romano or
    Parmesan cheese
1   cup shredded provolone or
    mozzarella cheese (4 ounces)
    Freshly ground pepper

Add cooking oil to a wok or large skillet. Preheat over medium-high heat (add more oil as necessary during cooking). Stir-fry garlic in hot oil for 15 seconds.

Add zucchini and yellow squash; stir-fry for 3 minutes. Add mushrooms and green onions; stir-fry about 1 minute more or till vegetables are crisp-tender. Add tomato, oregano, and ⅛ teaspoon pepper; stir-fry for 2 minutes more. Remove from heat.

Add hot cooked pasta and Romano or Parmesan cheese to vegetable mixture. Toss to combine. Serve immediately. Sprinkle with provolone or mozzarella cheese and freshly ground pepper. Makes 4 servings.

Nutrition information per serving: 412 calories, 19 g protein, 53 g carbohydrate, 14 g fat (7 g saturated fat), 27 mg cholesterol, 340 mg sodium.

Vegetarian Fried Rice

Transform fried rice from a side dish into a sumptuous meal by adding extra eggs and lots of vegetables.

5   slightly beaten eggs
1   tablespoon soy sauce
2   tablespoons cooking oil
1   small onion, chopped (⅓ cup)
1   clove garlic, minced
2   stalks celery, thinly bias-sliced
        (1 cup)
1½ cups sliced fresh mushrooms
1   medium green sweet pepper,
        chopped (¾ cup)
4   cups cold cooked rice
1   8-ounce can bamboo shoots,
        drained
2   medium carrots, shredded (1 cup)
¾   cup frozen peas, thawed
3   tablespoons soy sauce
3   green onions, sliced (⅓ cup)
     Crinkle-cut carrot slices (optional)

In a small bowl combine eggs and 1 tablespoon soy sauce. Set aside.

Add 1 tablespoon cooking oil to a wok or large skillet. Preheat over medium heat. Stir-fry chopped onion and garlic in hot oil about 2 minutes or till crisp-tender. Add the egg mixture and stir gently to scramble. When set, remove from wok. Cut up any large pieces of egg mixture. Let wok cool slightly.

Add remaining oil to cooled wok. Preheat over medium-high heat (add more oil if necessary during cooking). Stir-fry celery in hot oil for 1 minute. Add the mushrooms and green pepper; stir-fry for 1 to 2 minutes more or till vegetables are crisp-tender.

Add cooked rice, bamboo shoots, carrots, and peas. Sprinkle with 3 tablespoons soy sauce. Cook and stir for 4 to 6 minutes or till heated through. Add the cooked egg mixture and green onions. Cook and stir about 1 minute more or till heated through. Serve immediately. If desired, garnish with carrot slices. Makes 4 to 5 servings.

Nutrition information per serving: 438 calories, 17 g protein, 61 g carbohydrate, 14 g fat (3 g saturated fat), 266 mg cholesterol, 1,177 mg sodium.

INDEX